Better Homes and Gardens®

SAVORY SANDWICHES

Our seal assures you that every recipe in *Savory Sandwiches*
has been tested in the Better Homes and Gardens® Test Kitchen.
This means that each recipe is practical and reliable,
and meets our high standards of taste appeal.

For years, Better Homes and Gardens® Books has been a leader in publishing cook books. In *Savory Sandwiches,* we've pulled together a delicious collection of recipes from several of our latest best-sellers. These no-fail recipes will make your cooking easier and more enjoyable.

Editor: Rosemary C. Hutchinson
Editorial Project Manager: James D. Blume
Graphic Designer: Harijs Priekulis
Electronic Text Processor: Paula Forest

On the front cover: Chicken Salad Croissants *(see recipe, page 38)*

ISBN: 0-696-01718-0

Contents

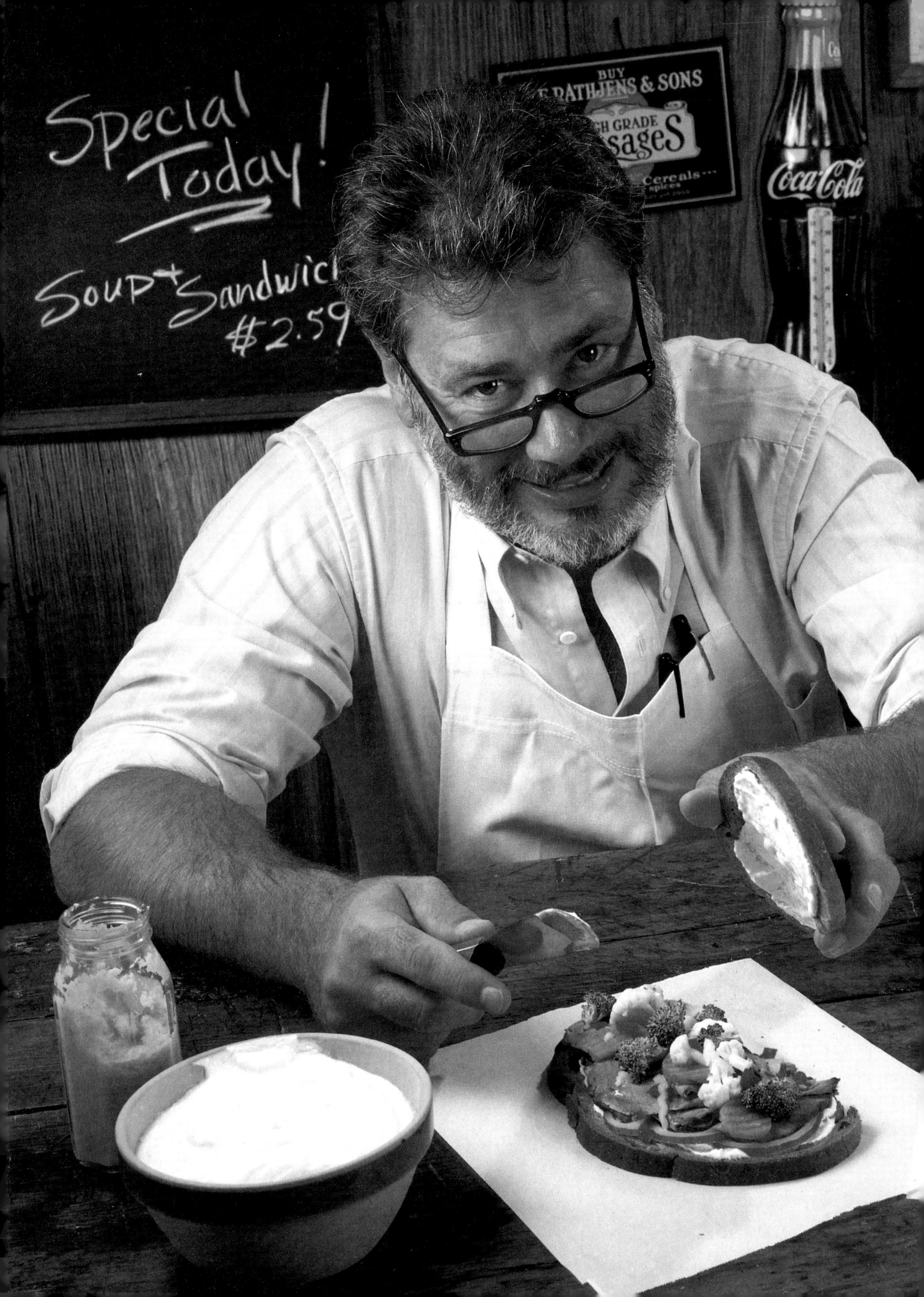
Special Today!
$2.59
BUY
Coca-Cola

Bavarian Beef Sandwiches

½ cup dairy sour cream
2 to 3 teaspoons prepared horseradish
8 slices pumpernickel bread

½ of a small onion, sliced and separated into rings (optional)
8 ounces thinly sliced cooked beef
1 pint marinated mixed vegetable salad, well drained

● In a small bowl stir together sour cream and horseradish. Spread one side of each of the bread slices with some of the sour cream mixture.

● If desired, place onion rings on the sour cream side of *four* bread slices. Top with beef. Cut up any large pieces of vegetable salad. Spoon atop beef. Top with remaining bread slices, sour cream side down. Makes 4 servings.

The sky's the limit when it comes to vegetable options for marinated salads. The version we found in the deli contained chunks of broccoli, cauliflower, and carrot. The version from your deli may be very different but just as tasty.

Coney Burgers

1 beaten egg
1 10-ounce can tomatoes
    and green chili peppers
2 tablespoons fine dry bread
    crumbs
½ teaspoon chili powder
1 pound lean ground beef
2 frankfurters

● In a medium mixing bowl combine egg, ¼ cup of the tomatoes and green chili peppers, bread crumbs, and chili powder. Add ground beef and mix well.

Cut frankfurters in half lengthwise. Shape ¼ of the meat mixture around *each* frankfurter half.

Place meat-wrapped frankfurters on an unheated rack in a broiler pan. Broil 4 to 5 inches from the heat for 8 to 10 minutes total or till done, turning once.

Mmm, mmm, mmm. There's nothing better than juicy burgers on crispy, toasted buns. To toast your frankfurter or hamburger buns, place them, cut side up, on the broiler rack around the burgers. Broil for 1 to 2 minutes, watching closely so the buns don't get too dark.

1 teaspoon cornstarch
1 teaspoon chili powder
1 8-ounce can red kidney
    beans, drained

● Meanwhile, in a small saucepan combine the remaining tomatoes and green chili peppers, cornstarch, and chili powder. Cook and stir till thickened and bubbly, then cook and stir for 2 minutes more. Stir in beans and heat through.

4 frankfurter buns, split and
    toasted
    Shredded cheddar cheese

● Serve meat-wrapped frankfurters in buns with bean mixture. Sprinkle with cheddar cheese. Makes 4 servings.

Frank Facts

Bet your guests two bits that they don't know all these frank facts!

● The guy who put the bun around the wiener came from St. Louis. A sausage vendor at the 1904 World's Fair furnished his customers with white gloves to make eating the hot wieners easier. Customers were to return the gloves, but most didn't. So, the vendor's brother-in-law, a baker, thought of placing the sausages in long, slender buns.

● Because dachshunds and franks are similar in shape, folks labeled them "dachshund sausages." An artist created talking sausage-shaped cartoon characters but finding dachshund hard to spell and even harder to say, he nicknamed his characters "hot dogs." Since then, the cartoon has disappeared but the name lives on.

Glazed Lamb Burgers

1 beaten egg
2 tablespoons plain yogurt
¼ cup fine dry bread crumbs
½ teaspoon dried mint, crushed
1 pound ground lamb

● In a medium bowl combine egg and yogurt. Stir in bread crumbs and mint. Add lamb and mix well. Shape meat mixture into four ¾-inch-thick patties.

Place patties on an unheated rack in a broiler pan. Broil 3 to 4 inches from heat to desired doneness, turning once (allow about 11 minutes total for medium). *Or,* grill patties, on an uncovered grill, directly over *medium-hot* coals to desired doneness, turning once (allow 10 to 12 minutes total for medium).

In these burgers, the lamb's sweetness is accented with mint and apple jelly.

¼ cup apple jelly
1 tablespoon chopped pecans
1 tablespoon lemon juice
¼ teaspoon ground cinnamon
4 lettuce leaves
4 hamburger buns, split and toasted

● Meanwhile, for glaze, combine apple jelly, pecans, lemon juice, and cinnamon. Spread glaze over burgers during the last minute of broiling or grilling.

Serve burgers on lettuce-lined buns. Makes 4 servings.

Lobster Cakes Diablo

1 beaten egg
½ cup finely crushed rich round crackers
1 teaspoon prepared mustard
¼ teaspoon ground red pepper
1 6½-ounce can lobster meat *or* one 6-ounce can crabmeat, drained, flaked, and cartilage removed
2 tablespoons cooking oil *or* shortening

● In a medium mixing bowl combine egg, crushed crackers, mustard, and red pepper. Add lobster or crabmeat and mix well. Shape lobster mixture into two ½- to ¾-inch-thick patties. Cover and chill patties for at least 30 minutes.

In a 10-inch skillet cook patties in hot oil or shortening over medium heat for 3 to 4 minutes on each side or till golden brown. Drain patties on paper towels.

Diablo **means "devil" in Spanish, but "spicy" in culinary lingo. The devilish seasonings in this fish patty are mustard and ground red pepper.**

2 lettuce leaves
2 whole wheat hamburger buns, split and toasted
2 tomato slices

● Serve patties on lettuce-lined buns with tomato slices. Makes 2 servings.

Fish Patties With Herbed Tartar Sauce

2 beaten eggs
⅓ cup fine dry bread crumbs
½ teaspoon dried oregano, crushed
¼ teaspoon dried basil, crushed
2 cups flaked, cooked fish
½ cup finely crushed rich round crackers (12 crackers)
2 tablespoons cooking oil *or* shortening

● In a medium mixing bowl combine eggs, bread crumbs, oregano, and basil. Add fish and mix well. Shape fish mixture into four ¾-inch-thick patties. Coat patties with crushed crackers (see photo, below).
　In a 10-inch skillet cook patties in hot oil or shortening over medium-low heat about 3 minutes on each side or till golden brown.

Leftover haddock or cod makes great patties.

4 hamburger buns, split and toasted
Herbed Tartar Sauce

● Serve patties on buns with Herbed Tartar Sauce. Makes 4 servings.

Herbed Tartar Sauce: In a small mixing bowl combine ¼ cup *dairy sour cream,* ¼ cup *mayonnaise or salad dressing,* 1 tablespoon snipped *parsley,* 1 tablespoon sliced *green onion,* 1 tablespoon finely chopped *sweet pickle,* ¼ teaspoon *dry mustard,* ¼ teaspoon *paprika,* ⅛ teaspoon *salt,* and dash *pepper.* Makes about ½ cup.

Flake cooked fish by inserting a fork at a 45-degree angle. Twist the fork gently and the fish will break apart easily.

Put crushed crackers in a shallow dish or on a piece of waxed paper. Place a fish patty in the crumbs and twist it gently so the crumbs stick to the bottom. Turn the patty over and twist it again. Repeat with the rest of the fish patties.

Sandwich Supper For Six

After a fun-filled day at the ballpark (or anyplace else), end with this impromptu dinner for six. On your way home, make a stop at the deli for the ingredients. Then pull them together for a meal that's sure to be a winner (see recipes, pages 12–13).

Sandwich Supper for Six

Menu

Potato-Salad-Ham Stack-Up

Deli cucumber salad

Potato chips

Lemon 'n' Tea Pitcher

Gingersnap Parfaits

Menu Countdown

45 Minutes Ahead:
Prepare Lemon 'n' Tea Pitcher; chill.
Assemble and chill Gingersnap Parfaits.

25 Minutes Ahead:
Prepare Potato-Salad-Ham Stack-Up.

Before Serving:
Put potato chips and cucumber salad in bowls.

Potato-Salad-Ham Stack-Up

Pictured on pages 10–11.

1 **16-ounce loaf unsliced French *or* Vienna bread (16 to 20 inches long)**
   Horseradish mustard
   Butter *or* margarine, softened

● With a sharp thin-bladed knife cut bread in half horizontally. Use a fork to hollow center of loaf bottom, leaving a $1/2$-inch shell. If desired, hollow top of bread. Spread cut side of loaf top with horseradish mustard. Spread cut side of loaf bottom with butter or margarine.

For individual sandwiches, use six 6-inch French-style rolls.

   Lettuce leaves
1 **pint German-style *or* mayonnaise-style potato salad**
8 **ounces sliced boiled ham *or* salami**
6 **slices Swiss cheese**
2 **medium tomatoes, thinly sliced**
   Sweet pickles (optional)
   Olives (optional)

● Layer lettuce, potato salad, ham or salami, cheese, and tomato slices over bottom of loaf. Place loaf top on sandwich. Secure sandwich with 6-inch skewers. Slice into 6 portions. If desired, garnish with pickles and olives. Serves 6.

Lemon 'n' Tea Pitcher

Pictured on pages 10–11.

6 cups water 5 bags mint-flavored tea	● In a saucepan bring water to boiling. Pour boiling water into a heat-proof pitcher. Add tea bags. Cover and let steep 3 to 5 minutes. Remove tea bags.

1 6-ounce envelope sugar-
  sweetened lemonade
  mix
  Ice cubes
	● Stir in lemonade mix. Cool. Add ice. Just before serving pour into glasses. Makes 6 (8-ounce) servings.

When the going gets tough, a pitcher of iced mint tea sweetened with lemonade saves the day.

Gingersnap Parfaits

Pictured on pages 10–11.

⅔ cup milk
2 1.4-ounce envelopes
  whipped dessert
  topping mix
2 tablespoons orange
  juice *or* liqueur
	● In a small mixer bowl stir together milk, topping mix, and orange juice or liqueur. Beat with an electric mixer on low speed till well combined. Beat at high speed about 2 minutes or till soft peaks form. Beat for 2 minutes more.

1 11-ounce can mandarin
  orange sections, drained
7 gingersnaps, coarsely
  crumbled
	● Reserve 6 mandarin orange sections. Reserve ⅓ *cup* of the topping mixture. Pipe or spoon remaining topping mixture into 6 parfait glasses.
	  Layer the remaining mandarin orange slices and gingersnaps into parfait glasses. Pipe or spoon reserved whipped topping mixture atop. Garnish with reserved mandarin orange sections. Chill in the freezer for 15 minutes. Makes 6 servings.

To save the hassle of whipping your own topper, use a 4-ounce container of frozen whipped dessert topping. Allow about 20 minutes for the topping to thaw. Then stir in the orange juice.

Tuna Canoes

¼ cup plain low-fat yogurt	● In a medium mixing bowl stir together yogurt, mayonnaise or salad dressing, mustard, dillweed, and pepper.
2 tablespoons mayonnaise *or* salad dressing	
1 teaspoon prepared mustard	
¼ teaspoon dried dillweed	
Dash pepper	

1 6½-ounce can tuna (water pack), drained and flaked	● Stir tuna and red pepper, carrot, or celery into yogurt mixture. Use a fork to hollow out the tops and bottoms of buns, leaving ¼-inch shells. Sprinkle cheese into hollowed-out bun halves. Spoon tuna mixture over cheese. Makes 4 sandwiches.
⅓ cup chopped red sweet pepper, carrot, *or* celery	
2 frankfurter buns, split	
½ cup shredded cheddar cheese (2 ounces)	

Sprinkle shredded cheese into the hollowed-out frankfurter buns. Then spoon the tuna mixture over the cheese. The cheese prevents the bread from getting soggy.

Curried Baloney Sandwiches

¼ cup plain low-fat yogurt	● In a small mixing bowl stir together yogurt, mayonnaise or salad dressing, and curry powder or mustard.
2 tablespoons mayonnaise *or* salad dressing	
¼ teaspoon curry powder *or* 1 teaspoon prepared mustard	

1 cup finely chopped bologna	● Stir bologna, carrot, raisins or currants, and celery into yogurt mixture. Spread butter on one side of each slice of bread. Spread bologna mixture on *half* of the bread slices. Top with remaining bread, butter side down. Halve sandwiches. Makes 3 sandwiches.
¼ cup shredded carrot	
¼ cup raisins *or* currants	
¼ cup chopped celery	
Butter *or* margarine	
6 slices whole grain bread	

For a super healthful sandwich, use turkey bologna. It has 33% less fat than beef or pork bologna.

Silhouette Sandwiches

1 **3-ounce package cream cheese, softened** **1** **tablespoon orange juice *or* milk**	● In a small mixer bowl beat *two-thirds* of the cream cheese and all of the orange juice with an electric mixer on low speed till smooth.
½ **cup diced fully cooked ham** **⅓** **cup shredded cheddar cheese** **2** **tablespoons finely chopped nuts**	● Add ham, cheese, and chopped nuts. Beat well. Store in a tightly covered container in the refrigerator for up to 3 weeks. (Soften before using.)
12 **slices whole wheat bread** **Finely chopped vegetables dried fruit, *or* nuts (optional)**	● For *each* of 6 sandwiches, use a cookie cutter to cut out a figure from *2 slices* of bread. Spread 1 figure with some of the ham mixture. Top with second figure. Use some of the remaining cheese, vegetables, fruit, or nuts to decorate the top, if desired. Makes 3 servings.

Create sandwiches of any shape you wish. Numbers, letters, animals' faces: let your imagination go wild.

Fill-Your-Pocket Pitas

What's to eat? Here's an easy, fun way to answer that question. Have everyone open their "pockets" (pocket bread, that is) and fill them full of cold cuts, vegetables, cheese strips, and other stuff from our mix-and-match chart. Plan on 1½ ounces of meat and cheese per pocket.

● Plan on *1 large pita bread round* for every *two* people. Cut the pita bread rounds crosswise in half. Open each bread half to form a pocket.
● Quarter the cold-cut slices.
● Prepare the vegetables.
● Assemble the greens.
● Cut the cheese into julienne strips.
● Arrange the filling ingredients on a platter. Set out the spreads.
● Let each person make his or her own sandwich by first spreading the inside of a pita pocket with one of the spreads, then filling it with cold cuts, veggies, greens, and cheese strips.

Spreads + Cold Cuts + Veggies + Greens

Spreads	Cold Cuts	Veggies	Greens
Mayonnaise or salad dressing	Sliced bologna	Thinly sliced carrots	Torn lettuce
Soft-style cream cheese	Sliced turkey or chicken breast	Sliced cucumber or zucchini	Thinly sliced celery
Butter or margarine, softened	Sliced boiled ham, honey loaf, or salami	Cherry tomatoes, cut in half	Chopped green pepper
		Pickle slices	Alfalfa sprouts

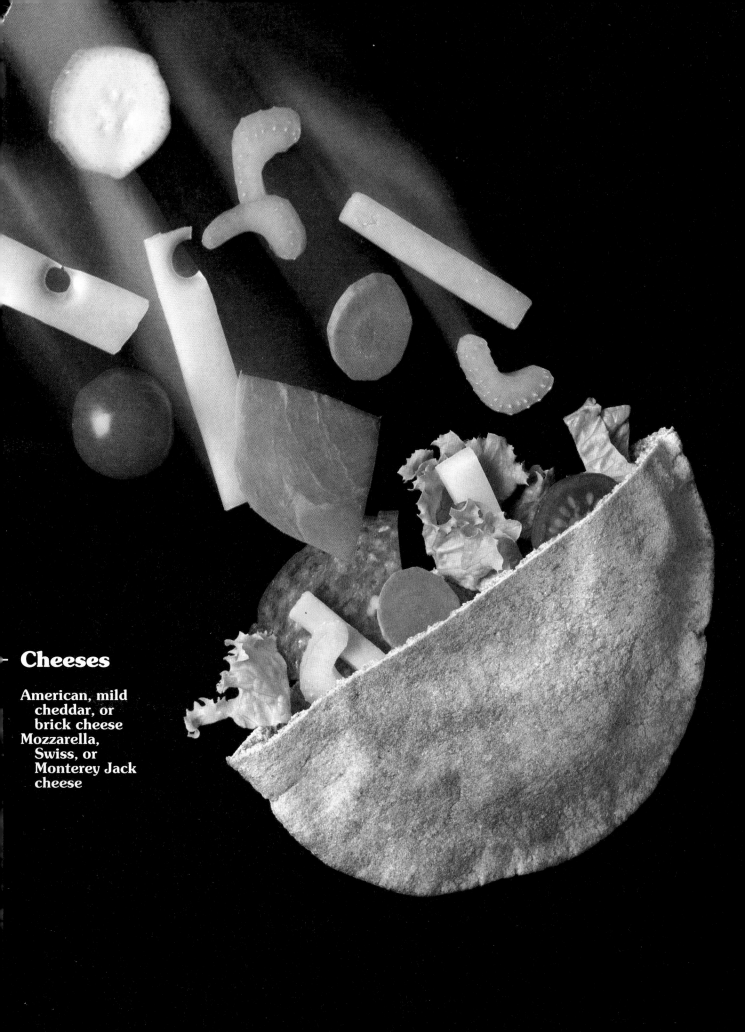

Cheeses

American, mild
cheddar, or
brick cheese
Mozzarella,
Swiss, or
Monterey Jack
cheese

Round burgers don't fit inside taco shells very well, so we made these burgers oval instead.

Pat the ground beef mixture into oval patties, making each patty about 5 inches long and ½ inch thick.

Taco Burgers

1 beaten egg
2 tablespoons catsup
¼ cup fine dry bread crumbs
1 to 1½ teaspoons chili powder
1 teaspoon Worcestershire sauce
½ teaspoon garlic salt
¼ teaspoon dry mustard
1 pound lean ground beef

● In a medium mixing bowl combine egg and catsup. Stir in bread crumbs, chili powder, Worcestershire sauce, garlic salt, and mustard. Add ground beef and mix well. Shape the ground beef mixture into 8 oval patties, each about 5 inches long and ½ inch thick.

Place patties on an unheated rack in a broiler pan. Broil 3 to 4 inches from the heat to desired doneness, turning once (allow about 9 minutes total for medium). *Or,* grill patties, on an uncovered grill, directly over *medium-hot* coals to desired doneness, turning once (allow 6 to 8 minutes total for medium).

8 taco shells
Shredded lettuce
Shredded cheddar *or* American cheese
Chopped tomato

● Serve burgers in taco shells with lettuce, cheese, and chopped tomato. Makes 4 servings.

Besides lettuce, cheese, and tomato, try topping your Taco Burgers with some sliced ripe olives, a dollop of sour cream, and taco sauce or salsa.

Shrimp Salad Pocket

2 ounces frozen cooked shrimp (½ cup)
2 tablespoons frozen peas
2 tablespoons chopped green sweet pepper
2 tablespoons creamy cucumber salad dressing
½ teaspoon lemon juice
⅛ teaspoon dried thyme, crushed

● Thaw and coarsely chop the frozen shrimp. Thaw the frozen peas. In a small mixing bowl combine the shrimp, peas, green pepper, cucumber salad dressing, lemon juice, and thyme. Stir mixture till well combined.

½ cup shredded lettuce
1 6-inch pita bread round

● Add lettuce to the shrimp mixture; toss to mix. Cut the pita bread in half, forming two pockets. Wrap and store one for another use. Spoon the shrimp mixture into the remaining pocket. Makes 1 sandwich.

Pack a pita full of this shrimp salad and be the envy of the office at lunchtime. Keep the filling separate from the bread and store it in a refrigerator at work till you're ready to eat. Or, place the filling in a vacuum bottle or insulated lunch box with a freezer pack before leaving home.

Herbed Veggie Burgers

3 cups water
¾ cup dry lentils

● In a medium saucepan bring water and lentils to boiling. Reduce the heat and simmer, covered, about 35 minutes or till tender. Drain and mash lentils.

2 beaten eggs
½ cup toasted pumpkin seed, chopped
½ cup fine dry bread crumbs
¼ cup chopped walnuts
¼ cup finely chopped green pepper
¼ cup finely chopped onion
¼ cup snipped parsley
½ teaspoon dried oregano, crushed
½ teaspoon dried basil, crushed
1 tablespoon butter or margarine
3 large whole wheat pita bread rounds, halved crosswise
6 tomato slices
   Alfalfa sprouts
   Dairy sour cream or plain yogurt (optional)

● In a medium mixing bowl combine eggs, pumpkin seed, bread crumbs, nuts, green pepper, onion, parsley, oregano, basil, ¼ teaspoon *salt*, ¼ teaspoon *pepper*, and mashed lentils. Shape the lentil mixture into 6 oval patties, each about 5 inches long and ½ inch thick.

In a 12-inch skillet cook patties in butter over medium-low heat about 4 minutes on each side or till golden brown.

Serve patties in pita halves with tomato slices, alfalfa sprouts, and sour cream or yogurt, if desired. Serves 6.

Snipping fresh herbs such as parsley is a snap. Just put the herb in a 1-cup measure and snip it with kitchen shears.

Sweet-and-Sour-Relish Burgers

2	slices bacon
⅓	cup chopped red *or* green sweet pepper
¼	cup chopped onion
1½	cups shredded cabbage
¼	cup shredded carrot
2	tablespoons brown sugar
2	tablespoons vinegar
2	tablespoons cold water
1	teaspoon cornstarch

● For relish, in a 10-inch skillet cook bacon till crisp. Drain bacon, reserving 1 tablespoon drippings. Crumble bacon.

In the skillet cook sweet pepper and onion in drippings till tender but not brown. Stir in cabbage, carrot, brown sugar, and vinegar. Cover and cook for 5 minutes. Combine water and cornstarch; add to skillet. Cook and stir till thickened and bubbly, then cook and stir 2 minutes more. Stir in bacon. Heat through.

1	pound ground pork *or* raw turkey
¼	teaspoon salt

● Meanwhile, for burgers, shape meat into 4 oval patties, each about 5 inches long and ½ inch thick. Sprinkle with salt.

Place patties on an unheated rack in a broiler pan. (Lightly grease rack if using turkey.) Broil 3 to 4 inches from the heat about 11 minutes total or till well-done, turning once. (Always cook pork and turkey till well-done.) *Or,* grill patties, on an uncovered grill, directly over *medium-hot* coals for 8 to 10 minutes total or till well-done, turning once. (Brush cold grill rack with cooking oil if using turkey.)

2	large pita bread rounds, halved crosswise

● Serve burgers in pita halves with relish. Makes 4 servings.

You can't fit a square peg into a round hole—or a round burger into an oblong pita bread pocket! To serve burgers in pita bread, shape the meat into oval patties about 5 inches long.

Hot Tuna Sandwich Cups

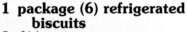

1 package (6) refrigerated biscuits
2 6½-ounce cans tuna (water pack), drained and flaked
½ cup shredded cheddar cheese (2 ounces)
1 medium green onion, sliced
¼ cup creamy buttermilk salad dressing
2 tablespoons sweet pickle relish

● Separate the biscuit dough into 6 biscuits. Grease the *outside* of six 6-ounce custard cups. Press 1 portion of dough around the outside of each custard cup, covering the bottom of the cup and halfway down the sides.

Place cups, dough side up, on an ungreased 15x10x1-inch baking pan. Bake in a 400° oven about 7 minutes or till light brown.

Meanwhile, in a medium mixing bowl stir together the tuna, cheese, onion, salad dressing, and pickle relish.

1. Press one biscuit around the outside of each greased custard cup.

● When biscuits are done, immediately remove them from custard cups and place them on a wire rack. Spoon some of the tuna mixture into each cup.

6 thin tomato slices
½ cup shredded cheddar cheese (2 ounces)
Celery leaves (optional)

● Place filled cups on a 15x10x1-inch baking pan. Bake in a 400° oven about 7 minutes or till filling is heated through. Place tomato slices on hot tuna filling. Sprinkle with cheese. Bake for 2 to 3 minutes more or till cheese melts. Trim with celery leaves, if desired. Makes 6.

2. Remove baked biscuits from custard cups. Place on a wire rack.

3. Spoon tuna mixture into biscuit cups.

4. Top with tomato slices. Sprinkle with cheese. Bake for 2 to 3 minutes more or till cheese melts.

French Bread Pizzas

1 15-ounce can pizza
    sauce
8 ounces turkey ham, cut
    into bite-size strips
½ teaspoon dried oregano,
    crushed
⅛ teaspoon garlic powder

● Preheat the broiler. Meanwhile, in a medium saucepan combine pizza sauce, turkey ham, oregano, and garlic powder. Cook, covered, over medium heat for 4 to 5 minutes or till mixture is heated through, stirring occasionally.

French bread "boats" make perfect crusts for these quick turkey ham-and-cheese pizzas.

1 16-ounce loaf unsliced
    French bread (14 to 16
    inches long)
1 12-ounce package
    shredded mozzarella
    cheese (3 cups)

● Slice French bread in half horizontally. Hollow out each half, leaving a ½- to ¾-inch shell. Place bread halves, cut side up, on a baking sheet. Sprinkle *one-fourth* of the cheese atop each bread half. Broil 4 to 5 inches from the heat for 2 to 4 minutes or till cheese melts.

1 small green pepper, cut
    into rings

● Spoon pizza sauce mixture into bread halves. Sprinkle with the remaining cheese and top with green pepper rings. Broil for 2 to 3 minutes or till cheese is melted and bubbly. Serve immediately. Makes 4 to 6 servings.

Pizza Miniwiches

1 tube refrigerated
    biscuits (6 biscuits)

● Prepare biscuits according to the package directions.

These miniwiches may be small, but they're packed with loads of taste.

⅓ cup chopped canned
    mushrooms, chopped
    green pepper,
    or sliced pimiento-
    stuffed olives
2 tablespoons pizza sauce

● In a small bowl combine mushrooms, green pepper, or olives, and pizza sauce.

6 slices Canadian-style
    bacon, halved
3 slices Swiss *or*
    American cheese,
    quartered, *or* 2 slices
    mozzarella cheese,
    cut in sixths (3 ounces)

● Cut biscuits in half. On one half of each biscuit place *two* bacon half-slices and some of the pizza sauce mixture. On the other half place *two* pieces of cheese.
    Place biscuit halves on a baking sheet. Bake in a 450° oven for 3 to 4 minutes or till cheese is melted and sauce is bubbly. Put cheese and bacon halves together. Makes 3 servings.

Freewheeling Sandwiches

3¼ cups all-purpose flour
2 packages active dry yeast
1 tablespoon caraway seed

2 cups milk
½ cup sugar
¼ cup shortening
2 eggs
4 cups rye flour
Filling ingredients

● In a large mixer bowl combine 2½ *cups* of the all-purpose flour with the yeast and caraway seed. Set aside.

● In saucepan heat milk, sugar, shortening, and 1 tablespoon *salt* just till warm (115° to 120°) and shortening is almost melted; stir constantly. Add to flour mixture; add eggs. Beat with electric mixer on low speed for ½ minute, scraping sides of bowl constantly. Beat 3 minutes on high speed.

Stir in rye flour. Stir in as much of the remaining all-purpose flour as you can mix in with a spoon. Turn out onto floured surface. Knead in enough of the remaining flour to make a moderately stiff dough that is smooth and elastic (6 to 8 minutes total). Shape into a ball. Place in greased bowl; turn once. Cover; refrigerate 3 to 24 hours.

When ready to use, remove dough from refrigerator; uncover and let stand 20 minutes. Divide dough into 24 pieces; form each into a smooth ball. On floured surface, roll or pat each into a 5-inch circle. Place about ⅓ cup desired filling on half of the circle; fold over other half and seal edges with tines of fork. Place on a greased baking sheet. Bake in a 375° oven for 15 to 18 minutes or till golden. Serve with mustard, if desired. Makes 24.

Thinking of having a party? These Freewheeling Sandwiches are just right for a hungry gang. Make the sandwich dough before the crowd arrives. Cover and regfrigerate it for up to a day. At party time, set out all the sandwich fixings and let everybody mix and match ingredients to build unique creations. (To season each sandwich start with ⅛ teaspoon dried herb.) The sandwiches are small, so plan on two or three per person. To identify sandwiches, carve the owner's initials into each sandwich before baking.

Shape dough into balls. On a lightly floured surface flatten into circles, using your fingers or a rolling pin.

FILLING INGREDIENTS
Choose several items from each category.
Meats:
Use diced cooked lamb or ham, cooked Italian sausage or ground beef, or diced pepperoni.
Cheeses:
Use diced American, brick, cheddar, Monterey Jack, mozzarella, Muenster, or Swiss cheese.
Vegetables:
Use shredded cabbage or carrot; chopped green pepper or mushrooms; sliced olives; or sliced halved zucchini or onion.
Dried Herbs:
Use basil, dillweed, mustard, marjoram, oregano, savory, or tarragon.

Plan on ⅓ cup filling for each sandwich. To make 24 sandwiches, choose 8 cups of ingredients from the list at left. (A pound of cooked meat yields 3 cups when chopped; a pound of ground meat yields 2 to 3 cups.)

Spicy Chicken Triangles

1¾ to 2 cups all-purpose
  flour
1 package active dry yeast
½ teaspoon chili powder
½ teaspoon salt
⅔ cup warm water
  (115° to 120°)
1 tablespoon cooking oil

● In a small mixer bowl combine ⅔ *cup* of the flour, the yeast, chili powder, and salt. Add warm water and cooking oil. Beat with an electric mixer on low speed for ½ minute, scraping sides of bowl. Beat on high speed for 3 minutes.

It's a blend of several spicy ingredients that gives these sandwich triangles a just-right hotness. Chili powder goes into the bread dough, which surrounds a cheesy chicken filling seasoned with garlic, coriander, and green chili peppers.

● With a spoon, stir in as much of the remaining flour as you can. On a floured surface knead in enough remaining flour to make a moderately stiff dough that is smooth and elastic (6 to 8 minutes). Shape into a ball. Place in a greased bowl; turn once. Cover and let rise in a warm place till double (about 1 hour).

½ cup chopped onion
¼ cup chopped green pepper
1 clove garlic, minced
½ teaspoon ground
  coriander
2 tablespoons butter *or*
  margarine
2 tablespoons tomato paste
¼ teaspoon salt

● Meanwhile, prepare the filling. In a skillet cook the onion, green pepper, garlic, and coriander in butter or margarine till the onion and green pepper are tender. Stir the tomato paste and salt into the cooked vegetable mixture.

1 cup chopped cooked
  chicken *or* turkey
1 8-ounce can whole kernel
  corn, drained
½ cup shredded Monterey
  Jack cheese (2 ounces)
½ of a 4-ounce can green
  chili peppers, rinsed,
  seeded, and chopped

● In a bowl combine the cooked chicken or turkey, corn, shredded Monterey Jack cheese, and green chili peppers. Add the cooked vegetable mixture; stir to mix well. Set the filling aside.

● Punch dough down; divide into 4 pieces. Cover; let rest 10 minutes. Roll each piece into a 6- to 8-inch square. Spoon about ½ *cup* of the filling atop each. Moisten the edges of the dough. Bring 2 opposite corners of each square together to form a triangle. With the tines of a fork, press edges together.

 Bake on a greased baking sheet in a 375° oven for 25 to 30 minutes. Serve warm. Makes 4 servings.

Poultry Bundles

1 package (8) refrigerated crescent rolls	● Unroll the crescent rolls; separate into 4 portions. Pinch perforations to seal.
2 5-ounce cans chunk-style chicken _or_ turkey, drained and chopped **½ cup shredded cheddar cheese (2 ounces)** **¼ cup snipped dried apricots** **¼ cup chopped pecans** **¼ teaspoon celery seed** **1 3-ounce package cream cheese, softened**	● In a bowl combine the chicken, cheddar cheese, apricots, pecans, and celery seed. Stir in the cream cheese. Spoon _one-fourth_ of mixture atop _each_ crescent roll rectangle. Bring the corners to the center atop filling; seal all the open edges (see photo, right). Moisten corners, if necessary.
	● Place each stuffed, sealed rectangle on a baking sheet. Bake in a 375° oven 12 to 15 minutes or till golden. Serve warm. Makes 4 sandwiches.

Here's how to keep the filling from leaking as the sandwiches bake: Top each rectangle of dough with the filling. Moisten the corners with water, if necessary. Bring the edges together atop the filling and pinch all the edges shut.

Ham and Swiss Packets

1 package (8) refrigerated crescent rolls	● Unroll the crescent rolls; separate into 4 portions. Pinch perforations to seal.
2 tablespoons applesauce **1 tablespoon orange marmalade** **1 cup shredded Swiss _or_ cheddar cheese (4 ounces)** **1 cup chopped fully cooked ham**	● In a bowl stir together the applesauce and marmalade. Stir in the cheese and ham. Spoon _one-fourth_ of the ham mixture atop _each_ crescent roll rectangle. Bring corners to center atop filling; seal all open edges (see photo, right). Moisten corners, if necessary.
	● Place each stuffed, sealed rectangle on a baking sheet. Bake in a 375° oven 12 to 15 minutes or till golden. Serve warm. Makes 4 sandwiches.

Unroll the
refrigerated dough.

Press two triangles
of dough together at the
perforations to form a
rectangle. You'll have 4
rectangles in all.

Salmon
Turnovers

These miniwiches may be
small, but they're packed
with taste.

½ of a stalk celery, chopped
1 green onion, sliced
1 tablespoon butter *or*
    margarine

● In a small skillet cook celery and onion in butter till celery is crisp-tender.

1 3-ounce package cream
    cheese, cut up
2 tablespoons snipped
    parsley
    Dash pepper
1 7¾-ounce can salmon,
    drained, skin and bones
    removed, and flaked

● In a small bowl stir together celery
mixture, cream cheese, parsley, and pepper till smooth. Fold in salmon.

1 package (8) refrigerated
    crescent rolls
    Milk
1 teaspoon poppy seed *or*
    sesame seed (optional)
    Parsley sprigs (optional)

● Unroll the crescent roll dough. Seal
perforations to form 4 rectangles. Pat
each into a 6x4½-inch rectangle. Place
¼ of the salmon mixture in center of
each rectangle. Fold the four points of
each rectangle over center. Pinch together edges to seal.

Place turnovers on an *ungreased* baking sheet. Brush with milk. If desired,
sprinkle with poppy seed or sesame
seed. Bake in a 375° oven for 12 to 15
minutes or till golden brown. Transfer to
a serving platter. Garnish with parsley, if
desired. Serve warm. Makes 4 servings.

Fold the four
corners of each
rectangle to the center.
Pinch seams together to
form a bundle.

Spoon ¼ cup of
the salmon mixture into
the center of each
rectangle.

Cheesy Pork Rounds

½ pound ground raw
 pork, beef, *or* turkey
¾ cup shredded American
 cheese (3 ounces)
1 small tomato, peeled,
 seeded, and chopped
 (½ cup)
2 tablespoons chopped
 sweet pickle

● In a 10-inch skillet cook and stir ground pork, beef, or turkey till meat is no longer pink. Drain. Stir in American cheese, tomato, and sweet pickle. Set mixture aside.

These rounds make great cold sandwiches, too. Just cool them on a wire rack. Then place them in a refrigerator bag and store them in the refrigerator for up to 3 days.

1 10-ounce package
 refrigerated hot loaf
1 beaten egg
1 teaspoon water

● Meanwhile, divide the dough into 8 pieces. On a lightly floured surface roll each piece into a 5-inch circle. In a small mixing bowl stir together the egg and water. Moisten the edges of dough circles with some of the egg mixture.

 Place about *½ cup* of the meat mixture onto *each* of *four* circles. Place remaining circles on top, egg side down, stretching to fit the bottom circles. Seal the edges (see photo, below).

● Place rounds on a greased baking sheet. Prick tops and brush with the remaining egg mixture. Bake in a 375° oven for 15 to 20 minutes or till golden. Remove from baking sheet. Serve warm. Makes 4 servings.

Use the tines of a fork to crimp the edges of the rounds.

Slumber Dogs

1 16-ounce loaf frozen
  bread dough, thawed
1 1-pound package (10)
  frankfurters
Prepared mustard
Catsup

● Divide dough into 10 portions. On a lightly floured surface roll out each portion into a 10x2½-inch rectangle.

Place a frankfurter lengthwise on each rectangle, about ¾ inch from one end. Spread frankfurter with mustard and catsup. Fold dough over to cover ¾ of the frankfurter. Moisten edges with water. Press together to seal.

Transfer to a greased baking sheet. Cover and let dough rise in a warm place for 30 minutes.

Bake in a 375° oven for 15 to 17 minutes or till golden brown.

Perfect for a slumber party, these dogs come with their own sleeping bags. Conquer the midnight hungries by adding some chips or popcorn, carrot or celery sticks, and milk, juice, or pop.

1 4⅝-ounce pressurized can
  cheddar cheese spread
Corn snack horns
Finely chopped green
  pepper
Pimiento pieces

● Cool slightly. To decorate, use cheese to make hair and to attach corn snack horns as hats. Attach green pepper to frankfurter for eyes and pimiento for mouth. Makes 10 servings.

Early-Morning Turnovers

1 package (6) refrigerated biscuits 3 1-ounce slices Canadian-style bacon 1 5-ounce jar cheese spread with pineapple	● On a floured surface roll each biscuit into a 5-inch circle. Place one slice of Canadian-style bacon on each of *three* dough rounds. Top each slice with *2 rounded tablespoons* of cheese spread. Moisten the edges of the dough rounds with water. Top with remaining dough rounds. Press edges together with your fingers, making fluted edges.	These breakfast sand-wiches make hefty fare for camping meals, too. Add them, frozen, to your cool-er in the evening just be-fore you go. They'll be thawed and ready to eat by morning.
Milk Sesame seed	● Brush the tops with milk; sprinkle with sesame seed. Place on an ungreased bak-ing sheet. Bake in a 450° oven for 14 to 16 minutes or till golden brown. Serve warm. Or, cool on a wire rack up to 1 hour. Pack each turnover in a small clear plastic bag or freezer bag. Store up to 1 week in the refrigerator or up to 1 month in the freezer. Makes 3 servings.	

Date-Nut Breakfast Bagels

1 3-ounce package cream cheese, softened 1 tablespoon orange juice 2 tablespoons snipped pitted whole dates 2 tablespoons chopped pecans	● In a small bowl stir together the soft-ened cream cheese and orange juice till smooth. Stir in the snipped dates and chopped pecans.	You can turn these bagel-wiches into grab-and-run morning meals. Just pack each sandwich in a small clear plastic bag or freez-er bag and store them up to a week in the refrigera-tor or up to a month in the freezer.
2 whole wheat *or* egg bagels, split	● Spread *half* of the cream cheese mix-ture onto the bottom half of *each* bagel. Top with remaining half. Makes 2.	

Breakfast Burgers

¾ **pound ground turkey sausage *or* bulk pork sausage**
3 **slices American cheese, quartered**

● Shape sausage into six ¼-inch-thick patties. Place patties on an unheated rack in a broiler pan. Broil 3 to 4 inches from the heat about 6 minutes total or till well-done, turning once. Top each burger with 2 cheese quarters. Heat just till cheese melts.

3 **eggs**
2 **tablespoons milk**
⅛ **teaspoon salt**
   Dash pepper
1 **tablespoon butter *or* margarine**
6 **Cornmeal-Herb Biscuits *or* toasted English muffins, split**

● Meanwhile, in a small bowl beat together eggs, milk, salt, and pepper.
   In an 8-inch skillet cook and stir eggs in hot butter or margarine, cooking just till set. Place some of the scrambled eggs atop each biscuit or muffin bottom. Top with burgers and biscuit or muffin tops. Makes 6 servings.

Cornmeal-Herb Biscuits: In a medium mixing bowl stir together 1 cup *all-purpose flour,* ¼ cup *yellow cornmeal,* 1½ teaspoons *baking powder,* ¼ teaspoon *salt,* ¼ teaspoon *baking soda,* and ¼ teaspoon dried *oregano, basil, or marjoram,* crushed.
   In a small mixing bowl combine one 8-ounce carton dairy *sour cream* and 2 tablespoons *milk.* Make a well in the center of the dry ingredients, then add sour cream mixture. Stir just till the dough clings together.
   Knead gently on a lightly floured surface for 10 to 12 strokes. Roll or pat to a ½-inch thickness. Cut with a 3-inch biscuit cutter, rerolling as necessary.
   Transfer to a lightly greased baking sheet. Bake in a 375° oven about 18 minutes or till golden. Makes 6 biscuits.

Kneading 10 to 12 strokes—no less and no more—is the secret to turning out first-rate biscuits every time. Too little kneading turns out biscuits that are small and round; the other extreme gives you biscuits that are tough and dry, with peaks on top.

Chicken Salad Croissants

Also pictured on the cover.

1 **8-ounce can crushed pineapple (juice pack)**	● For dressing, in a small saucepan combine the *undrained* pineapple, cornstarch, ginger, and salt. Cook and stir over medium heat till thickened and bubbly. Cook and stir 2 minutes more. Cool. Add the mayonnaise or salad dressing. Stir to mix well.
1 **teaspoon cornstarch**	
¼ **teaspoon ground ginger**	
¼ **teaspoon salt**	
⅓ **cup mayonnaise *or* salad dressing**	
1 **cup chopped cooked chicken**	● In a small bowl combine the chicken, green pepper, and almonds. Add the pineapple dressing; stir to mix well. Divide between 2 small airtight containers. Store up to 1 week in the refrigerator. Makes enough filling for 2 sandwiches.
¼ **cup chopped green pepper**	
¼ **cup sliced almonds, toasted**	
Whole wheat *or* white croissants, split	● For *each* serving, in the morning pack *one* whole wheat or white croissant and a *small amount* of Bibb lettuce or *one* lettuce leaf in separate small clear plastic bags. Carry with *1 container* of the chilled chicken mixture in an insulated lunch box with a frozen ice pack.
Bibb lettuce *or* lettuce leaves	
	At lunchtime, assemble the croissant, the lettuce, and the chicken salad mixture into a sandwich.

The pineapple and ginger flavors in this filling go well with a wide selection of breads, from croissants to whole wheat slices.

Turkey-Relish Supreme

1 **5-ounce can chunk-style turkey *or* chicken, drained and chopped**	● In a bowl combine the turkey or chicken, cranberry relish, Swiss or cheddar cheese, mayonnaise or salad dressing, celery, and pecans. Stir to mix well.
¼ **cup cranberry-orange relish**	
¼ **cup shredded Swiss *or* cheddar cheese (1 ounce)**	Divide between 2 small airtight containers. Store the mixture up to 1 week in the refrigerator. Makes enough filling for 2 sandwiches.
3 **tablespoons mayonnaise *or* salad dressing**	
2 **tablespoons finely chopped celery**	
2 **tablespoons chopped pecans**	
Sandwich bread	● For *each* serving, in the morning pack *2 slices* of bread and *one* lettuce leaf in separate small clear plastic bags. Carry with *1 container* of the chilled turkey mixture in an insulated lunch box with a frozen ice pack.
Lettuce leaves	
	At lunchtime, assemble the bread, lettuce leaf, and the turkey-relish mixture into a sandwich.

All insulated containers are not alike. Thick mixtures like this filling stay colder longer in an insulated lunch box with a frozen ice pack. Use insulated vacuum bottles when you want to keep saucier mixtures such as soups hot or cold.

Plan an elegant lunch with a friend, and take Chicken Salad Croissants. Just put *all* of the chicken mixture into *one* airtight container before chilling. Take *two* croissants and extra lettuce. For dessert, include in-season fresh fruit. Add bright paper napkins, and you're ready for lunchtime entertaining. (Don't forget a spoon for assembling the sandwiches.)

Peanut Butter-Pineapple Deluxe

⅔ cup chunk-style peanut
   butter
½ of a 3-ounce package
   cream cheese, softened
½ cup drained crushed
   pineapple
¼ cup shredded carrot
8 slices sandwich bread

● In a small bowl stir together the peanut butter and softened cream cheese. Stir in the pineapple and carrot.
   Spread mixture on *4 slices* of the sandwich bread. Top with remaining slices. Pack each sandwich in a freezer bag. Store up to 1 month in the freezer. Makes 4 sandwiches.

Don't skip peanut butter sandwiches just because they stick to the roof of your mouth. Try this flavorful concoction! Cream cheese and pineapple add to the flavor and make the peanut butter easier to eat, too.

Lettuce leaves

● For *each* serving, in the morning pack *one* lettuce leaf in a small clear plastic bag. Carry lettuce with *1 frozen* sandwich in a brown bag with a frozen ice pack. The sandwich will thaw in 4 to 6 hours.
   At lunchtime, add lettuce to sandwich.

Peanut Butter Sunshine Sandwiches (see recipe, page 43)

Peanutty Baconwiches

½ cup chunk-style peanut
    butter
2 tablespoons mayonnaise
    or salad dressing
1 medium tomato, peeled,
    seeded, and chopped
¼ cup cooked bacon pieces
2 tablespoons sweet pickle
    relish
1 tablespoon finely chopped
    onion (optional)

● In a bowl combine the chunk-style peanut butter and the mayonnaise or salad dressing. Stir to mix well.

Stir in the chopped tomato, cooked bacon pieces, sweet pickle relish, and the finely chopped onion, if desired. Pack in a small airtight container. Store up to 1 week in the refrigerator. Makes enough spread for 3 sandwiches.

Here's a savory peanut butter spread for more sophisticated tastes. It makes a deliciously extraordinary sandwich.

Sandwich bread

● For *each* serving, in the morning use *⅓ cup chilled* spread and *2 slices* bread to make a sandwich. Pack in a small clear plastic bag. Carry in an insulated lunch box with a frozen ice pack.

Salmon-Stuffed French Rolls

½ cup chopped broccoli *or* cauliflower flowerets
¼ cup shredded carrot
¼ cup chopped cucumber

● In a bowl toss together the chopped broccoli or cauliflower flowerets, shredded carrot, and chopped cucumber.

⅓ cup mayonnaise *or* salad dressing
½ teaspoon dried dillweed
⅛ teaspoon pepper
1 7¾-ounce can salmon, drained, slightly flaked, and skin and bones removed

● Stir in the mayonnaise or salad dressing, dillweed, and pepper. Fold in the flaked salmon. Divide among 3 small airtight containers. Store mixture up to 1 week in the refrigerator. Makes enough filling for 3 sandwiches.

French-style rolls, split, *or* sandwich bread
Green pepper rings

● For *each* serving, in the morning pack *one* roll or *2 slices* of bread and *two or three* green pepper rings in separate clear plastic bags. Carry roll or bread and green pepper with *1 container* of the chilled salmon mixture in an insulated lunch box with a frozen ice pack.

At lunchtime, assemble the roll or bread, the salmon mixture, and the green pepper into a sandwich.

Vary the flavor of this or just about any of our other terrific sandwich fillings by layering different vegetables in your sandwich. Try sliced radishes, tomato slices, bean sprouts, cucumber slices, shredded carrot, or thinly sliced green onion in place of (or in addition to) the green pepper rings. Just pack the vegetables in a small clear plastic bag, and add them to your sandwich at lunchtime.

Hot Dog Pockets

½ cup baked beans
1 frankfurter, sliced crosswise
¼ cup shredded American cheese (1 ounce)
2 tablespoons sweet French salad dressing
1 tablespoon finely chopped onion

● In a small bowl stir together the baked beans, frankfurter slices, American cheese, French salad dressing, and onion. Pack in an airtight container. Store mixture up to 1 week in the refrigerator. Makes enough filling for 1 sandwich.

1 large pita bread round, split crosswise
2 lettuce leaves

● For 1 serving, in the morning pack the pita halves and lettuce in separate small clear plastic bags. Carry with the chilled baked bean mixture in an insulated lunch box with a frozen ice pack.

At lunchtime, line each pita pocket with a lettuce leaf. Spoon *half* of the baked bean filling into each pocket.

Please kids of all ages with this hearty hot dog and bean combo. Pita bread "pockets" neatly hold the saucy filling.

Peanut Butter Sunshine Sandwiches

Pictured on page 40.

¾ **cup chunk-style peanut butter**	● In a small bowl combine the peanut butter and the orange juice. Stir till well mixed. Stir in the raisins. Pack in an airtight container. Store up to 1 month in the refrigerator. Makes enough spread for 3 sandwiches.
¼ **cup orange juice**	
⅓ **cup chopped raisins**	
Sandwich bread	● For *each* serving, in the morning spread about ⅓ *cup* of peanut butter mixture onto *1 slice* of bread. Top with *another slice.* Pack in a small clear plastic bag. Carry in a brown bag.

For quick packing later, make three sandwiches at once. Wrap them in freezer bags and store up to one month in the freezer.

Cheesy BLTs

½ **cup cream-style cottage cheese, drained**	● Press drained cottage cheese through a sieve into a medium bowl (see photo, right). Add the softened cream cheese, the American cheese, and hot pepper sauce. Stir till well mixed. Stir in the bacon and tomato. Pack in an airtight container. Store up to 1 week in the refrigerator. Makes enough spread for 3 or 4 sandwiches.
1 **3-ounce package cream cheese with chives, softened**	
¼ **cup shredded American cheese (1 ounce)**	
Several dashes bottled hot pepper sauce	
6 **slices bacon, crisp-cooked, drained, and crumbled**	
1 **medium tomato, seeded and chopped**	
Sandwich bread	● For *each* serving, in the morning spread about ⅓ *to* ½ *cup* of the chilled mixture onto *1 slice* of sandwich bread; top with *another slice* of bread. Pack in a small clear plastic bag. Pack lettuce leaves in a separate plastic bag. Carry sandwich and lettuce in an insulated lunch box with a frozen ice pack.
Lettuce leaves	

Use the back of a large spoon to gently press the drained cottage cheese through a sieve.

Walnut-Fruit Sandwiches

½ teaspoon finely shredded
   orange peel
½ cup orange juice
¾ cup walnuts
⅓ cup dried apples
⅓ cup pitted dates
⅓ cup raisins

● In a blender container or food processor bowl combine the orange peel and orange juice. Add the walnuts, dried apples, dates, and raisins. Cover and process till nearly smooth, about 2 minutes, stopping to scrape sides, if necessary. Divide mixture between 2 small airtight containers. Store up to 3 weeks in the refrigerator. Makes enough for 2 servings.

For hectic days when your appetite demands an extra-filling lunch, pack this richly satisfying walnut butter. Spread it thickly, making two open-face sandwiches at lunchtime.

Sandwich bread

● For *each* serving, in the morning pack *2 slices* of bread in a small clear plastic bag. Carry the bread with *1 container* of the walnut mixture in a brown bag.
   At lunchtime, spread *half* of the walnut mixture onto *each* slice of bread.

Mediterranean Sandwiches

1 15-ounce can garbanzo beans, drained	● In a blender container or food processor bowl combine the drained garbanzo beans, tahini, lemon juice, garlic, salt, and paprika. Cover and process till smooth, stopping to scrape sides, if necessary. Stir in the parsley and pimiento.
¼ cup tahini (sesame seed paste)	
3 tablespoons lemon juice	
2 cloves garlic, minced	
½ teaspoon salt	
¼ teaspoon paprika	
½ cup snipped parsley	
1 2-ounce jar pimiento, drained and chopped	
5 bagels, split	● Spread about ⅓ cup of the mixture onto the bottom half of each bagel. Add bagel top. Pack each sandwich in a freezer bag. Store sandwiches up to 1 month in the freezer. Makes 5 sandwiches.
	● For each serving, in the morning pack 1 frozen sandwich in a brown bag. Sandwich will thaw at room temperature in 4 to 6 hours.

Tahini, or sesame seed paste, is available in Oriental markets and in some large grocery stores.

Or, you can easily make your own in a blender: Process ½ cup *sesame seed*, covered, in a blender or a food processor fitted with a steel blade until the seed is the consistency of a fine powder. Add 2 tablespoons *cooking oil*. Cover and process till smooth. Makes ¼ cup.

Double-Cheese Hamwiches

½ cup shredded cheddar cheese (2 ounces)	● In a small bowl stir together the shredded cheddar cheese, softened cream cheese, and brown or Dijon-style mustard. Stir in the cut-up smoked ham and chopped sweet pickle or pickle relish.
1 3-ounce package cream cheese, softened	
2 teaspoons brown *or* Dijon-style mustard	
1 2½-ounce package very thinly sliced smoked ham, cut up	
2 tablespoons chopped sweet pickle *or* sweet pickle relish	
6 slices sandwich bread	● Spread *one-third* of the mixture onto each of *3 slices* of bread. Top with remaining slices. Pack each sandwich in a freezer bag. Store up to 1 month in the freezer. Makes 3 sandwiches.
Lettuce leaves	● For each serving, in the morning pack a lettuce leaf in a small clear plastic bag. Carry the lettuce leaf with 1 frozen sandwich in an insulated lunch box with a frozen ice pack.
	At lunchtime, add the lettuce leaf to the sandwich.

Packing the lettuce leaf in a separate bag helps keep it crisp.

Robot Rounds

1 **10-ounce package refrigerated hot loaf**	● Divide dough into 8 pieces. On a floured surface roll each piece into a 5-inch circle. In a small bowl stir together egg and water. Moisten edges of dough circles with some of the egg mixture.
1 **beaten egg**	
1 **teaspoon water**	

1 **2½- to 3-ounce package very thinly sliced corned beef, chopped**	● For filling, in a small bowl toss together corned beef and cheese. Spread some of the mustard over *each* circle. Place about ½ cup of the filling onto *each* of *four* circles. Place remaining circles, mustard side down, on top, stretching to fit bottom circles. Seal edges, using the tines of a fork.
1½ **cups shredded Swiss cheese (6 ounces)**	
1 **tablespoon horseradish mustard *or* prepared mustard**	

● Place rounds on a greased baking sheet. Prick tops and brush with the remaining egg mixture. Bake in a 375° oven for 15 to 20 minutes or till golden. Remove rounds from baking sheet. Cool on a wire rack. Place each sandwich in a freezer bag. Store up to 1 month in the freezer. Makes 4 sandwiches.

● For *each* serving, in the morning pack *1 frozen* round in a brown bag. Sandwich will thaw at room temperature in about 4 hours.

Turkey Robot Rounds: Prepare as above *except,* omit filling and mustard. Instead, on the center of *each* of 4 circles place 1 slice of *American cheese,* tearing to fit. Then add *one-fourth* of a 2½- to 3-ounce package *very thinly sliced turkey or chicken.* Add 3 *dill or sweet pickle slices* and 1 slice of process *Swiss cheese,* tearing it to fit. Top with remaining dough circles, egg side down, and continue as above. Makes 4.

Lunching space trekkers throughout the universe will eagerly volunteer to discover what cosmic wonders are sealed in these turnovers.

Index